GW00726961

To:

_____

From:

_____

THE GIFT
of
READING

THE GIFT
of
READING

MICHAEL O'MARA BOOKS LIMITED

First published in Great Britain
in 2009 by
Michael O'Mara Books Limited
9 Lion Yard
Tremadoc Road
London SW4 7NQ

A CIP catalogue record for this book
is available from the British Library.

ISBN: 978-1-84317-410-3

1 2 3 4 5 6 7 8 9 10

www.mombooks.com

Printed and bound in China
by WKT

'There is no greater gift one can give to a child than the love of reading.'

MARGARET SOPER

MISTAKES OF BIBLICAL PROPORTIONS

Of all books that have ever been printed, the Bible is the most popular, selling in the millions. However, what is less well known is that there have been many editions of the Bible, within which terrible printers errors have occurred. For instance, in 1631 the 'Adulterers' Bible' appeared, in which Exodus 20:14 read: 'Thou shalt commit adultery'. In 1716 the 'Sin On' Bible was printed, where John 5:14, reads, 'sin on more', instead of 'sin no more'. Following on from this there is the 'Vinegar Bible' of 1717, where Luke 20 reads, 'The Parable of the

Vinegar' – instead of 'Vineyard'.
In the same vein, we also have the
'Wicked Bible', the 'Wife-hater
Bible', the 'Treacle Bible', the 'Idle
Bible' and the 'Murderer's Bible',
amongst others.

❧

*'Read. Do not brood. Immerse
yourself in long study: only the habit
of persistent work can make one
continually content; it produces an
opium that numbs the soul.'*

GUSTAVE FLAUBERT IN A LETTER
TO LOUISE COLET, 1851

MISTAKEN ENTHUSIASM!

American novelist James Carroll recorded the following anecdote having visited the works that was printing his most recent book.

'My host and tour guide, a Little, Brown executive, showed me the assembly line along which workers wrapped, boxed, and mailed off books to wholesalers and bookstores. At one point he introduced me to one of the workers who said, "Mr Carroll, we all just love your book."

'I took that as the greatest compliment an author could receive: to think that these workers had actually troubled to

read my book.

But then she went on, "We just love it. It's the perfect size for packing."'

WORLD'S MOST EXPENSIVE BOOK

A British entrepreneur, Roger Shashoua, is the mastermind behind what is thought to be the world's most expensive book, which is a blow-by-blow account of how Shashoua made his fortune doing business in post-Soviet Russia.

Each of the made-to-order volumes in the special edition boasts a cover containing 600 diamonds and it is aimed at Russian oligarchs who can obviously afford such luxuries.

'One would need a heart of stone to read the death of Little Nell without laughing.'
OSCAR WILDE

THE GREAT LIBRARY OF ALEXANDRIA

Perhaps the most famous library of them all was the one founded in Alexandria by Ptolomy I Soter, circa 230 BC. Said to contain

up 700,000 papyrus scrolls, the library was seen as a collection of the world's knowledge and covered every subject from medicine to astrology, engineering, physics, literature, mathematics, philosophy and languages, to name but a few.

Sadly, the library was destroyed – although how and when is disputed. Some historians point the finger at Julius Caesar, who was said to have set the place on fire, others are less clear as to the culprit. Whatever the case, the library disappeared and nowadays nothing remains but its ghost.

ETERNITY

The German novelist and essayist Thomas Mann was a stickler for getting his books just right before they were published, and consequently made alterations to his manuscripts right up until the last minute. However, when he wrote *The Magic Mountain*, a book of some considerable length, his publisher lost patience with the author, shouting, 'We'll never get this book out! You've been working on it for eternity!'

Calmly, Mann replied, 'After all, I am writing it for eternity!'

'Every man who knows how to read has it in his power to magnify himself, to multiply the ways in which he exists, to make his life full, significant and interesting.'

ALDOUS HUXLEY

BESTSELLERS

Bestsellers are not a new phenomenon, although one might think they are given the press coverage that the Harry Potter books garner. When Charles Dickens wrote *The Old Curiosity Shop* in 1841, it was initially published in serial form both in

Britain and in the United States. In
fact, so huge was the readership in
the States that when the fate of the
heroine, Little Nell, was thought
to hang in the balance, the docks
in New York were crowded with
desperate readers all clamouring
to find out whether she was going
to live or die!

ADVENTURES WITH BOOKS

*Books are ships that sail the seas
To lands of snow or jungle trees
And I'm the captain bold and free
Who will decide which
place we'll see
Come let us sail the magic ship.*

Books are trains in many lands
Crossing hills or desert sands
And I'm the engineer who guides
The train on its exciting rides.
Come, let us ride the magic train.

Books are zoos that make a home
For birds and beasts
not free to roam
And I'm the keeper of the zoo
I choose the things to show to you
Come, let us visit in a zoo.

Books are gardens, fairies, elves
Cowboys and people like ourselves
And I can find with one good look
Just what I want inside a book
Come, let us read!
For reading's fun.

ANONYMOUS

THE NOBEL PRIZE

Awarded since 1901, the Nobel Prize honours men and women from all over the world for outstanding achievements in physics, chemistry, medicine, literature and for work for peace.

The prize was established by scientist, inventor, author and pacifist Alfred Nobel, and Nobel laureates are nominated by their peers, with the Nobel Committee sending letters to selected nominators.

In literature, Nobel laureates have ranged from poets and novelists such as Rudyard Kipling (awarded 1907) to historians and biographers such as Winston Churchill (1953), to dramatists

such as Luigi Pirandello (1934). Recent laureates include Seamus Heaney, V.S. Naipaul, J.M. Coetzee, Harold Pinter and Doris Lessing.

DON'T INTERRUPT!

It can be very annoying when someone interrupts you while you are reading, but take pity on the American novelist Rex Stout (creator of the detective Nero Wolfe), whose parents were huge book enthusiasts. Stout's father had a library that contained over a thousand volumes and Stout's mother – who had nine children – loved nothing better than to spend her days reading, so much so, in

fact, that she kept a **large** basin of cold water and a **fla**nnel by her chair so that any **child** who dared interrupt her would **have** his or her face scrubbed!

GOOD OLD GBS

Eminent playwright George Bernard Shaw once **gave** a copy of one of his books to **an** old friend, signing it:

To………………

With esteem
George Bernard Shaw

Shaw then forgot about the gift. However, a few years later, while

rifling through the bookcases in a second-hand bookshop, he came across the volume he had given his friend. Shaw bought the book and returned it to his friend with a slightly amended inscription:

To.................

With *renewed* esteem
George Bernard Shaw

'I have somewhere seen it observed that we should make the same use of a book that the bee does of a flower; she steals sweets from it, but does not injure it.'

CHARLES C. COULTON

SCANDALOUS BOOKS

Originally published in Italy in 1928, D.H. Lawrence's *Lady Chatterley's Lover* is perhaps the most famous book to have caused a scandal. However, several other less likely titles have also caused controversy, such as Mary Shelley's *Frankenstein*, which was reported by *The New York Times* as being banned in South Africa during the apartheid regime for being 'indecent, objectionable or obscene'.

Similarly, Jack London's *The Call of the Wild* was banned in Yugoslavia for being 'too radical', and Walt Whitman's *Leaves of*

Grass was denied publication in the United States for a time due to its 'vulgarity' of language and subject matter. J.D. Salinger's *The Catcher in the Rye* was also deemed to be unsuitable for the general public to read due to its use of unsavoury language.

Most recently, Salman Rushdie's novel *The Satanic Verses,* published in 1988, caused an extreme reaction among some Muslim communities who were incensed by the author's portrayal of the Prophet Muhammad. Not only did they burn the book, but Iranian religious authorities also put out a *fatwa* on the author, causing Rushdie to go into hiding for several years.

DEFINITION OF A BOOKWORM

Bookworm – a grub that eats holes in books, esp. a beetle larva (*Anobium*); a hard reader.

CHAMBERS TWENTIETH-CENTURY DICTIONARY

POUND FOR POUND UNSOLD

Known for his hot-headedness, the poet Ezra Pound was one day involved in an argument with Lascelles Abercrombie, a professor of English Literature at Leeds University. Abercrombie had adamantly disagreed with a view that Pound had expressed,

prompting the poet to write him letter in which he said: 'Dear Mr Abercrombie, Stupidity carried beyond a certain point becomes a public menace. I hereby challenge you to a duel, to be fought at the earliest moment that is suited to your convenience…'

Understandably, Abercrombie was a little distressed at the thought of having to fight Pound – particularly as Pound was renowned for his skill at fencing. But then he recalled that the choice of weapons was actually his, so he replied to Pound by saying: 'May I suggest that we bombard each other with unsold copies of our own books?'

Pound, having a lot of unsold copies of his work, immediately

withdrew his challenge and the
duel never took place.

*What really knocks me out is a
book that, when you're all done
reading it, you wish the author that
wrote it was a terrific friend of yours
and you could call him up on the
phone whenever you felt like it.'*

J.D. SALINGER

'The books that the world
calls immoral are the
books that show the
world its own shame.'
OSCAR WILDE

A LITTLE BIT SLOW?

This anecdote was told by Nunnally Johnson, who wrote the script for the film *Along Came Jones*, which was produced by and starred Gary Cooper. Lending Cooper the novel upon which the film was based, some weeks later Johnson asked the famous actor how he was enjoying the novel.

'Oh, fine,' Cooper is said to have replied. 'I'm about halfway through. I'm reading it word by word.'

THE CELSUS LIBRARY
AT EPHESUS

Constructed circa AD 110 by
Gaius Julius Aquila in memory
of his father, Tiberius Julius
Celsus Polemaenus – this
extraordinary library is
believed to have contained over
12,000 handwritten books and
manuscripts. Sadly, much like the
library at Alexandria, the building
and all its contents were destroyed
by fire in the third century AD.

HOW CAN BOOKS SAVE THE WORLD?

Books cannot be killed by fire.
People die, but books never die.
No man and no force can abolish
memory… In this war, we know,
books are weapons. And it is a
part of your dedication always
to make them weapons for man's
freedom.
'Message to the Booksellers
of America – 6 May 1942' by
President Franklin D. Roosevelt

WORLD'S OLDEST BOOK

In May 2003 what is thought to be the world's oldest multiple-page book went on display at the National History Museum, Sofia, Bulgaria. Believed to be more than two-and-a-half millennia old (dating it back to 600 BC), the book was first discovered in the 1940s in a tomb in south-west Bulgaria. Written in the lost language of Etruscan, the manuscript contains six delicately bound sheets of exquisitely crafted 24-carat gold, depicting a mermaid, a harp, a horse and soldiers.

YOU'RE RIGHT, MR PRESIDENT

The thirtieth President of the United States, (John) Calvin Coolidge, loved reading but when his wife was persuaded to buy a very expensive medical almanac from a travelling salesman one day, he was less than impressed, and pretended not to notice the book. Several days later, when Mrs Coolidge opened it up, she noticed that her husband had written inside: 'This work suggests there is no cure for a sucker.'

A LITTLE LEARNING

Below are some useful examples of
little rhymes that can be incredibly
useful when you are learning your
alphabet or trying to figure out
how to remember other important
facts and figures that will come in
handy throughout your lifetime.

Roman figures

X shall stand for playmates Ten;
V for Five stout stalwart men;
I for One, as I'm alive;
C for a Hundred, and D for Five
   (hundred);
M for a Thousand soldiers true,
And L for Fifty, I'll tell you.

The alphabet

A, B, C, D, E, F, G,
Little Robin Redbreast sitting
  on a tree;
H, I, J, K, L, M, N,
He made love to little Jenny Wren;
O, P, Q, R, S, T, U,
Dear little Jenny, I want to
  marry you.
V, W, X, Y, Z
Poor little Jenny she blushed
  quite red.

Four memorable dates

William the Conqueror,
ten sixty-six,
Played on the Saxons
oft-cruel tricks.

In fourteen hundred and ninety-two
Columbus sailed the ocean blue.

•

The Spanish Armada met its fate
In fifteen hundred and eighty-eight.

•

In sixteen hundred and sixty-six,
London burnt like rotten sticks.

*'The things I want to know are in
books; my best friend is the man
who'll get me a book I ain't read.'*

ABRAHAM LINCOLN

WORLD'S BOOKIEST TOWN

Hay-on-Wye has to be the world's most book-infested town. Located on the Welsh side of the Welsh/English border in the county of Powys, there are an estimated thirty second-hand and antiquarian bookshops in this tiny metropolis, attracting hundreds of thousands of book enthusiasts every year. The Hay-on-Wye Literary Festival is known worldwide and usually takes place in May each year.

WELL SAID!

There is a story that an American general once asked Winston Churchill to look over the draft of an address he had written. It was returned with the comment, 'Too many passives and too many zeds.' The general asked Churchill what he meant, and was told, 'Too many Latinate polysyllabics like "systematize", "prioritize" and "finalize". And then the passives. What if I had said, instead of "We shall fight them on the beaches," "Hostilities will be engaged with our adversary on the coastal perimeter"?'

NAUGHTY EDITION

When Mark Twain's novel *Huckleberry Finn* was being prepared for printing a very mischievous engraver decided to play a joke. He cleverly altered one of the illustrations – adding a male sex organ to a drawing of Silas Phelps and thus changing the meaning of the illustration's caption, which had Aunt Sally asking: 'Who do you think it is?'

Unfortunately for the printers, the alteration wasn't discovered until thousands of printed sheets had come off the press and been collated and bound, after which the offending plate had to be cut out of each edition by hand!

'I've travelled the world twice over,
Met the famous; saints and sinners,
Poets and artists, kings and queens,
Old stars and hopeful beginners.
I've been where no one's
been before,
Learned secrets from writers
and cooks,
All on one library ticket,
To the wonderful world of books.'

ANONYMOUS

IMPOVERISHED

US statesman, author and scientist Benjamin Franklin was dining in Paris one day when the conversation among the dinner guests turned to 'What condition of man most deserves pity?' In turn, each of the diners gave an example of what he thought applied, until it came to Franklin's turn. He stated in no uncertain terms, 'A lonesome man on a rainy day who does not know how to read.'

USEFUL MNEMONICS

The definition of mnemonics is
'a process – usually employing
a short verse – to help us to
remember things.'

Which is bigger, India or Africa?

India's big, but Africa's bigger,
The same as their elephants – easy
to figure!

Points on the compass

Never Eat Shredded Wheat
(North, East, South, West)

The number of days in the months

Thirty days have September,
April, June and November.
All the rest have thirty-one
Excepting February alone;
Which has but twenty-eight in fine,
Till leap year gives it twenty-nine.

The planets in order of distance from the sun

My Very Earnest Mother Just
Served Us Nine (Pickles)
(Mercury, Venus, Earth, Mars,
Jupiter, Saturn, Uranus, Neptune,
{Pluto, now defined as a 'dwarf'
planet}).

THE SYLVIA BEACH LIBRARY

In 1919 a bookshop called Shakespeare & Company opened on the rue de l'Odéon in Paris. It was owned and run by a young American woman called Sylvia Beach, who had first come to Paris to study French literature.

Soon the bookshop became a Mecca for all the young writers of the period (especially young Americans and Englishmen) who had come to Paris for its bohemian atmosphere: Ernest Hemingway, F. Scott Fitzgerald and James Joyce were among the most famous. But it was Joyce who really put the bookshop on the literary map for,

having written *Ulysses*, he couldn't find a publisher willing to print it due to the very strict obscenity laws in England at this time. Undaunted by this, however, in 1922 Sylvia Beach offered to print the book under the Shakespeare & Company imprint.

Sadly, Shakespeare & Company had to close at rue de l'Odéon during World War II and Sylvia Beach died in 1962. But that wasn't the end of the bookshop, which reopened under new ownership on the rue de la Bucherie, opposite Notre-Dame Cathedral where, on going up some extremely rickety stairs one can still, if invited, view Syliva Beach's private library.

'The book is the greatest interactive
medium of all time. You can
underline it, write in the margins,
fold down a page, skip ahead and
you can take it anywhere.'

MICHAEL LYNTON – ON TAKING OVER
PENGUIN BOOKS, 1996

'If you can read this,
thank a teacher.'
ANONYMOUS

*'The founding of a library is one
of the greatest things we can do …
It is one of the quietest things; but
there is nothing that I know of at
bottom more important. Everyone
able to read a good book becomes
a wiser man. He becomes a similar
centre of light and order, and just
insight into the things around him.
A collection of good books contains
all of the nobleness and wisdom of
the world before us. A collection of
books is the best of all universities.'*

THOMAS CARLYLE

'Beware of the man with
only one book.'
ANONYMOUS

A WRITER'S LOT IS
NOT A HAPPY ONE

One night French novelist and
playwright Honoré de Balzac was
lying in bed when a thief broke
into the room. Watching him,
Balzac saw the man head straight
for his writing desk, where he tried
to pry open a drawer by picking
the lock. Balzac chuckled – and
the noise duly stopped the thief in
his tracks.

'Why are you laughing?' asked the rogue.

'I am laughing, my good fellow,' replied Balzac, 'to think what pains and risks you are taking in the hope of finding money by night in a desk where the lawful owner can never find any by day.'

> 'The more that you read, the more things you will know. The more that you learn, the more places you'll go.'
> DR SEUSS

PUBLISH AND BE DAMNED

Not every book that has been published has been greeted with enthusiasm. In recent memory *The Satanic Verses* by Salman Rushdie was met with severe opposition but it wasn't the first book to be blighted by disapproval.

After Thomas Hardy published *Jude the Obscure* in 1896, there was such an outcry at the subject matter that one bishop took it upon himself to burn the book as a sign of his disgust. Hardy took the action well, saying that the bishop was obviously furious 'presumably, at not being able to burn me'. However, after the furor died

down, Hardy decided never to write another novel and thereafter stuck to poetry, which was a great loss to lovers of his beautiful prose.

PAPER CUTS

In Hollywood in the 1930s there were only two movie gossip columnists whose opinions mattered: Hedda Hopper and Louella Parsons. With a combined readership said to be over 75 million people, they could make or break a young star or starlet's career with one acerbic swipe. Sam Goldwyn once quipped that 'Louella is stronger than Samson. He needed two columns to bring down the house. Louella can do it with one.'

'Some books are to be tasted, others to be swallowed, and some few to be chewed and digested.'
FRANCIS BACON

HOW MANY WORDS?

On meeting eminent American novelist and screenwriter Joel Sayre at a book reading one day, a young woman posed him a question.

'Mr Sayre, please can you tell me how many words there are in a novel?'

Sayre was rather nonplussed by the question, but nevertheless smiled and gave an answer. 'It depends,' he replied. 'A short novel would probably consist of about 65,000 words.'

'So, you're telling me that 65,000 words make a novel?'

'I suppose so,' said Sayre, fearing the worst.

'That's marvellous, then,' beamed the young woman. 'My book is finished!'

'Books say: she did this because. Life says: she did this. Books are where things are explained to you; life is where things aren't … Books make sense of life. The only problem is that the lives they make sense of are other people's lives, never your own.'

JULIAN BARNES

Mother: Bobby's teacher says he ought to have an encyclopaedia.
Father: Let him walk to school like I had to!

THE BODLEIAN LIBRARY

Situated in Oxford and established in 1598 by Sir Thomas Bodley around a previous library housed above the Old Congregation House, itself built in 1320, the Bodleian was opened to students in 1602 and is one of the oldest libraries in Europe. One of its many traditions, still upheld today, is that none of the library's books are allowed to leave the building; in fact even King Charles I was refused permission to borrow one. In 1914 the number of books in the library grew to over a million. A copyright library, it is second in size only to the British Library.

✿

*'Child! Do not throw this
book about;
Refrain from the unholy pleasure
Of cutting all the pictures out!
Preserve it as your chiefest
treasure.'*

HILLAIRE BELLOC

✿

THE DEFINITION
OF BOOKISH

Of, relating to, or resembling a
book; fond of books; studious.

BOOK DEDICATIONS

It has often been said that there should be a book dedicated to book dedications because there is definitely an art to writing a good, amusing one – just as there is an art to writing an amusing acceptance speech. One of the better book dedications is printed below and comes from the pen of that most English of authors, P. G. Wodehouse:

'To my daughter, Leonora, without whose never-failing sympathy and encouragement this book would have been finished in half the time.'

OUCH!

Book critics are often referred to by novelists as an unnecessary evil – but of course some are more evil than others … And then there are the novelists turned critic who can be the most evil of all. Consider the following examples:

Evelyn Waugh on Stephen Spender

To see him fumbling with our rich and delicate language is to experience all the horror of seeing a Sèvres vase in the hands of a chimpanzee.

Oscar Wilde on George Meredith

His style is chaos illuminate by flashes of lightning. As a writer he has mastered everything except language: as a novelist he can do everything except tell a story: as an artist he is everything except articulate.

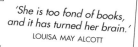

'She is too fond of books, and it has turned her brain.'
LOUISA MAY ALCOTT

WORLD BOOK DAY

The origins of World Book Day are said to lie in Catalonia where, on St George's Day, it has been the tradition for the past eight years or so to present loved ones with roses and books.

Now, World Book Day is an international festival that takes place in March every year and is celebrated in over 100 countries around the world.

In particular the day itself, which has been sanctioned by UNESCO (the United Nations Educational, Scientific and Cultural Organization), is not only a worldwide celebration of books but it is also a way of encouraging children to explore books more

fully, engage with them, and
generally discover the pleasures
and opportunities contained
within them.

'A dose of poison can do its
work but once, but a bad
book can go on poisoning
minds for generations.'
W. JOHN MURRAY

SPONGES, SAND-GLASSES, STRAIN-BAGS AND DIAMONDS

Readers may be divided into four classes:

1. Sponges, who absorb all that they read and return it in nearly the same state, only a little dirtied.

2. Sand-glasses, who retain nothing and are content to get through a book for the sake of getting through time.

3. Strain-bags, who retain merely the dregs of what they read.

4. Moghul diamonds, equally rare and valuable, who profit by what they read, and enable others to profit by it also.

SAMUEL TAYLOR COLERIDGE

'I have always imagined that paradise will be some kind of library!'
JORGE LUIS BORGES

THE MAN
BOOKER PRIZE

One of the most prestigious literary prizes in the world, the Man Booker Prize is now over forty years old. Started in 1969, the first novel to win was *Something To Answer For* by P. H. Newby (published by Faber and Faber).

The prize has courted much controversy over the years, particularly among different judging panels who never seem to fail to disagree vehemently about one book or another. One book that hasn't been tarred with this brush, however, was Salman Rushdie's *Midnight's Children*, which not only won the prize in

1981 but also went on to win the Booker of Booker's in 1993 and the Best of the Booker in 2008.

BOOKISH PHRASES

Bring someone to book

◆

Play it by the book

◆

Take a leaf out of my book

◆

Throw the book at you

◆

You can't judge a book
by it's cover

◆

You're in my bad books

BIBLIOGRAPHY

Braude, Jacob, *Braude's Handbook of Stories for Toastmasters and Speakers*, Prentice Hall, Inc, 1980

Fadiman, Clifton (ed), *The Faber Book of Anecdotes*, Faber and Faber, 1985

Fuller, Nigel, *2,500 Anecdotes for All Occasions*, Avenel Books, 1980

Knowles, Elizabeth (ed), *The Oxford Dictionary of Quotations*, Oxford University Press, 2001

Opie, Iona and Peter, *The Oxford Nursery Rhyme Book*, Oxford

University Press, 1973

Rees, Nigel, *Cassell Dictionary of Anecdotes*, Cassell, 2000

Rees, Nigel, *The Guinness Book of Humorous Anecdotes*, Guinness Publishing Ltd, 1994

Metcalf, Fred (ed), *The Penguin Dictionary of Modern Humorous Quotations*, Penguin 1986

WEBSITES

www.anecdotage.com

readinglady.com

news.bbc.co.uk

www.themanbookerprize.com

ALSO AVAILABLE IN THIS SERIES:

A Gift for Christmas
978-1-84317-408-0

♦

A Gift for Your Birthday
978-1-84317-409-7

♦

The Gift Book
978-1-84317-407-3

♦

The Gift for Girls
978-1-84317-424-0

♦

The Gift for Boys
978-1-84317-423-3